Bric & Stones

Skill Level

BEGINNER

Quilt Size
56" x 80"

Block Size
12" x 12"

Number of Blocks
24

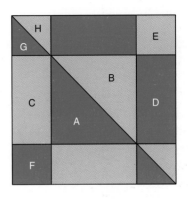

Bric & Stones
12" x 12" Finished Block
Make 24

Materials

- 42/45"-wide cotton quilting fabric*
    - 3¼ yards dark
    - 2¾ yards light
- Backing 4½ yards*
- Batting 64" x 88"*
- Thread to match fabric for piecing*
- Quilting thread*
- Walking or even-feed presser foot
- Basic sewing tools and supplies

Bali Batiks from Hoffman Fabrics; Deluxe Loft 100% Cotton Batting from Quilter's Dream; Soft Touch 60wt Long Staple Egyptian Cotton thread from YLI used to make sample.

Project Notes

Refer to the video for more detailed instructions and tips on all construction techniques.

Stitch ¼-inch seam allowances with right sides together unless otherwise instructed.

Cutting

Refer to the video for rotary cutting techniques and tips to cut the total number of pieces listed for each piece. Cutting instructions assume rotary cutting techniques will be used.

From light fabric:

- Cut 3 (6⅞" by fabric width) strips.
    - Subcut strips into 12 (6⅞") squares. Cut each square on one diagonal to make 24 B triangles.
- Cut 4 (6½" by fabric width) strips.
    - Subcut strips into 48 (3½" x 6½") C rectangles.
- Cut two (3½" by fabric width) strips.
    - Subcut strips into 24 (3½") E squares.
- Cut 3 (3⅞" by fabric width) strips.
    - Subcut strips into 24 (3⅞") squares. Cut each square on one diagonal to make 48 H triangles.
- Cut 7 (1½" by fabric width) I/J border strips. ***Note:*** *If you want to add a third color to your quilt, cut the I/J border strips from ½ yard of a color complimentary with the dark fabric referring to the video.*

From dark fabric:

- Cut 3 (6⅞" by fabric width) strips.
  Subcut strips into 12 (6⅞") squares. Cut each square on one diagonal to make 24 A triangles.
- Cut 4 (6½" by fabric width) strips.
  Subcut strips into 48 (3½" x 6½") D rectangles.
- Cut two (3½" by fabric width) strips.
  Subcut strips into 24 (3½") F squares.
- Cut 3 (3⅞" by fabric width) strips.
  Subcut strips into 24 (3⅞") squares. Cut each square on one diagonal to make 48 G triangles.
- Cut 7 (3½" by fabric width) K/L border strips.
- Cut 8 (2¼" by fabric width) strips for binding.

Completing the Blocks

1. Match A and B triangles right sides together. Carefully stitch A and B triangles together along longest side to make an A-B unit (Figure 1). Refer to video to chain-piece 24 A-B half-square units.

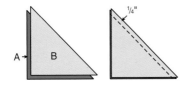

Figure 1

2. Press seam allowances toward A, referring to video and Figure 2. Trim dog ears from unit corners referring again to Figure 2.

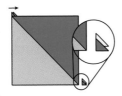

Figure 2

3. Repeat steps 1 and 2 with H and G triangles to make 48 H-G half-square units.

4. Referring to Figure 3, stitch the G side of an H-G unit to one short end of a C rectangle. Stitch an F square to opposite end. Press seams toward C, referring to the arrows in Figure 3, to make a block Top Row.

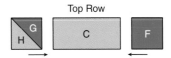

Figure 3

5. Stitch D to the B side of an A-B unit and C to the A side referring to Figure 4. Press seams toward C and D to make a block Center Row.

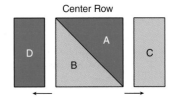

Figure 4

6. Stitch an E and H-G unit to opposite short sides of D to make a Bottom Row referring to Figure 5. Press seams toward D.

Figure 5

7. Stitch Top Row to Center Row matching C to A side of A-B unit and nesting seams referring to the video and Figure 6. Press seams toward center row.

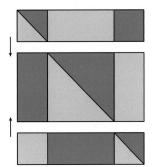

Figure 6

8. Stitch Bottom Row to Center Row matching D to B side of A-B unit and nesting seams referring again to the video and Figure 6. Press seam toward Center Row to complete one Bric & Stones block referring to the block diagram.

9. Repeat steps 4–8 referring to the video for chain-piecing tips to make 24 Bric & Stones blocks.

Completing the Rows

1. Refer to the Assembly Diagram, Figure 7 and the video to arrange four blocks into a row. Press seams to the left. Repeat to make three of Row 1.

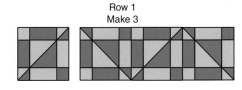

Row 1
Make 3

Figure 7

2. Refer to the Assembly Diagram, Figure 8 and the video to arrange four blocks into a second row layout. Press seams to the right. Repeat to make three of Row 2.

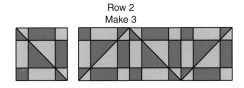

Row 2
Make 3

Figure 8

3. Stitch the rows together beginning with Row 1 and alternating with Row 2 matching seams and referring to Figure 9 and the video. The quilt top pieced center should measure 48½" x 72½".

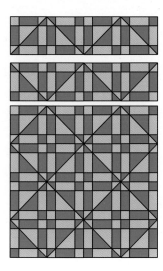

Figure 9

Adding Borders

1. Stitch the I/J border strips together using a diagonal seam as shown in the video.

2. Measure through the center of the pieced quilt center from top to bottom for the side borders. Measure through the center of the pieced quilt center from side to side for the top/bottom borders, and add twice the width of the border you are adding minus 1". For this quilt, the J side border measurement should be 72½". The I top/bottom border measurement should be 48½" + 3" - 1" = 50½".

3. Stitch the J borders to opposite long sides of the quilt top (Figure 10). Press the seams toward J.

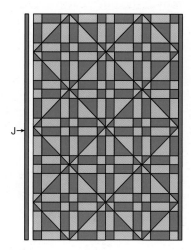

Figure 10

4. Stitch the I borders to the top and bottom of the quilt top (Figure 11). Press seams toward I.

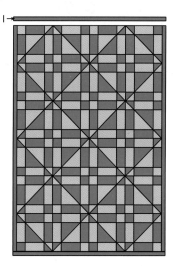

Figure 11

5. Prepare and stitch K/L borders to the quilt top referring to steps 1–4, the video and the Assembly Diagram.

Preparing a Quilt Sandwich & Quilting

1. Square up the quilt top by measuring the middle, top and bottom of the quilt width and length referring to Figure 12 and the video. Correct any discrepancies using your ruler and rotary blade.

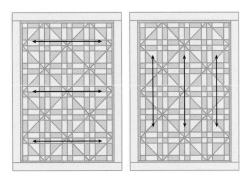

Figure 12

2. Yardages are given in the Materials List for piecing the quilt backing. Refer to the video for removing the backing selvages and piecing techniques. Make sure your backing is at least 4" larger on all sides than the quilt top.

3. Press out any wrinkles and fold lines in the backing. Press piecing seams open. Apply sizing or spray starch to the wrong side if desired.

4. Layer the quilt backing wrong side up, and the batting and quilt top right side up to make a quilt sandwich referring to Figure 13 and the video.

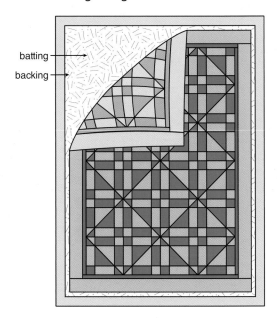

batting

backing

Figure 13

5. Secure the layers together with curved quilter's safety pins working from the center out and pinning every 4" referring again to the video.

6. Determine how to quilt the quilt sandwich referring to the video for suggestions on stitch-in-the-ditch and using quilting stencil designs.

7. Prepare you sewing machine to quilt by attaching an even-feed or walking presser foot, a new quilting needle and threading with chosen quilting thread.

8. Divide the quilt into sections and begin quilting at the center of the quilt working out. To help manage the quilt bulk in the machine throat, roll that section of the quilt toward the needle.

9. Work in one section at a time. When turning, leave the needle down, raise the presser foot and pivot the quilt in the desired direction. Take your time.

10. To secure the stitches at the beginning and end of a section, backstitch two to three stitches.

11. Refer to the video for more detailed instructions and tips on making a quilt sandwich, choosing and marking a quilting pattern, and stitching.

Binding Your Quilt

1. Stitch the binding strips together using a diagonal seam, trim seam allowance to ¼" and press open referring to Figure 14 and the video.

2. Press the binding in half lengthwise referring again to Figure 14.

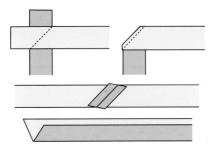

Figure 14

3. Beginning in the middle of one long side, pin the binding strip to the quilt top matching raw edges to the first corner (Figure 15). Begin stitching approximately 12" from the beginning end of binding.

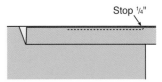

Stop ¼"

Figure 15

4. Stop stitching ¼" from the corner. With needle down, rotate the quilt and stitch off the quilt corner at a 45-degree angle to the seam.

5. Remove the quilt from the machine. Fold the binding up along the 45-degree stitching line and then down even with quilt edges, forming a pleat at corner, referring to Figure 16.

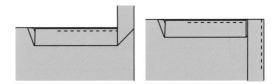

Figure 16

6. Resume stitching from corner edge as shown in Figure 16, down quilt side stopping stitching ¼" from next corner.

7. Repeat steps 4–6 to miter all corners. Stop stitching approximately 12" from the beginning of stitching.

8. Position the binding end over the beginning and pin mark (Figure 17). Measure over 2¼" toward the binding edge and trim the beginning end.

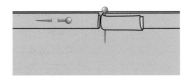

Figure 17

9. Open the binding ends flat. Position the binding ends right sides together and stitch a diagonal seam referring to Figure 18. Trim the seam allowance and press open. Refold the binding in half (Figure 19).

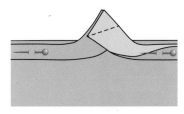

Figure 18

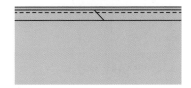

Figure 19

10. Complete stitching the binding in place, backstitching at the end of stitching to secure.

11. Fold binding to the quilt back and hand-stitch in place. Take a few stitches at each mitered corner to hold the corner folds in place.

12. Refer to the video for more detailed instructions and tips on preparing the binding, mitering binding corners, joining the binding ends, and stitching the binding to the quilt back. ●

Alternate-Size Quilts

Yardages for Alternate-Size Quilts

Pattern download instructions are written for a twin-size quilt (56" x 80"). Alternate sizes are listed below with number of blocks required for each size and yardages for quilt top fabrics 42/45" wide. Adjust border widths on double- to king-size quilts to achieve the overall quilt size listed. Refer to video for instructions on determining batting and backing sizes and amounts.

Cut individual pieces listed in download Cutting instructions to make the number of blocks needed for each size referring to list below. Refer to the video for instructions on measuring and cutting border and binding strips for alternate sizes.

	Quilt Size	# Blocks	Dark Fabric	Light Fabric
Bed Runner	80" x 32"	12 blocks	2 yards	1⅜ yards
Wall Hanging	44" x 44"	9 blocks	2 yards	1⅛ yards
Baby Quilt	44" x 56"	12 blocks	2⅛ yards	1½ yards
Double	70" x 82"	30 blocks	3⅞ yards	3 yards
Queen	82" x 94"	42 blocks	4¾ yards	3⅞ yards
King	94" x 106"	56 blocks	6 yards	5 yards

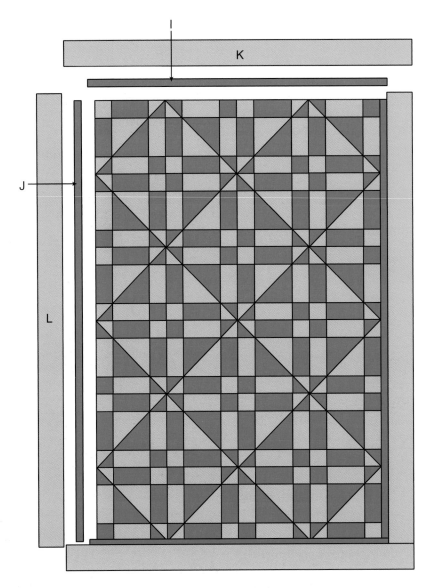

Bric & Stones
Assembly Diagram 56" x 80"

Alternate Colors

Alternate Block Layouts

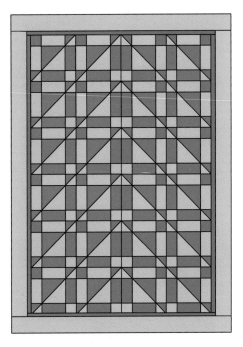

Chevrons Bed Quilt
Alternate Placement Diagram 56" x 80"

Diamond With Chevrons Bed Quilt
Alternate Placement Diagram 56" x 80"

Large Diamonds Bed Quilt
Alternate Placement Diagram 56" x 80"

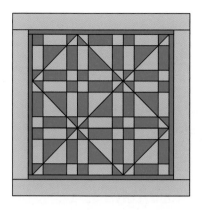

Bric & Stones Wall Hanging
Alternate Placement Diagram 44" x 44"

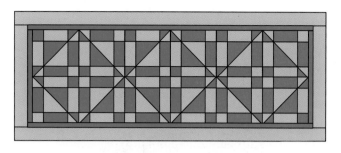

Bric & Stones Bed Runner
Alternate Placement Diagram 80" x 32"

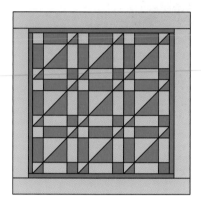

Same Direction Wall Hanging
Placement Diagram 44" x 44"

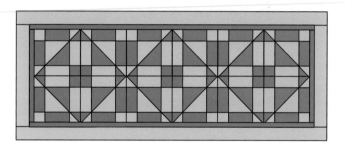

Large Diamonds Bed Runner
Alternate Placement Diagram 80" x 32"

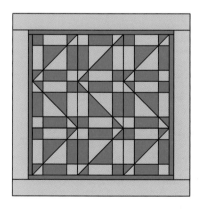

Zigzag Wall Hanging
Alternate Placement Diagram 44" x 44"

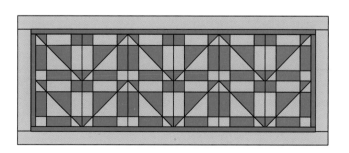

Zigzag Bed Runner
Alternate Placement Diagram 80" x 32"

Quilting Terms

Appliqué: Adding fabric motifs to a foundation fabric by hand or machine.

Basting: Temporarily secures layers of quilting materials together with safety pins, thread or a spray adhesive in preparation for quilting the layers.

Uses a long, straight stitch to hand- or machine-stitch one element to another holding the elements in place during construction and is usually removed after construction.

Batting: An insulating material made in a variety of fiber contents that is used between the quilt top and back to provide extra warmth and loft or protection from heat in kitchen accessories.

Binding: A finishing strip of fabric sewn to the outer raw edges of a quilt to cover them.

Straight-grain binding strips, cut on the crosswise straight grain of the fabric (see Straight & Bias Grain Lines illustration), are commonly used.

Bias binding strips are cut at a 45-degree angle to the straight grain of the fabric. They are used when binding is being added to curved edges.

Block: The basic quilting unit that is repeated to complete the quilt's design composition. Blocks can be pieced, appliquéd or solid and are usually square or rectangular in shape.

BOM: Common abbreviation for block of the month.

Border: The frame of a quilt's central design used to visually complete the design and give the eye a place to rest.

Dog Ears: Seam-allowance points that extend beyond block or quit top edges after pieces are stitched and pressed. Trim to match edges and reduce seam- allowance bulk.

Fabric Grain: The fibers that run either parallel (lengthwise grain) or perpendicular (crosswise grain) to the fabric selvage are straight grain.

Bias is any diagonal line between the lengthwise or crosswise grain. At these angles the fabric is less stable and stretches easily. The true bias of a woven fabric is a 45-degree angle between the lengthwise and crosswise grain lines.

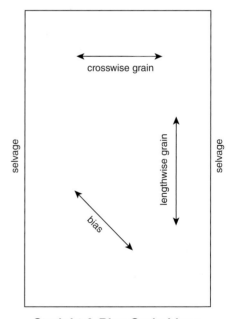

Straight & Bias Grain Lines

HST: Common abbreviation for half-square triangle.

Mitered Corners: Matching borders or turning bindings at a 45-degree angle at corners.

Nesting Seams: By pressing seam allowances in opposite directions in blocks or rows, the seams can be butted against each other, or nested, and matched more easily.

Patchwork: A general term for the completed blocks or quilts that are made from smaller shapes sewn together.

Pattern: This may refer to the design of a fabric or to the written instructions for a particular quilt design.

Piecing: The act of sewing smaller pieces and/or units of a block or quilt together. Paper or foundation piecing is sewing fabric to a paper or cloth foundation in a certain order.

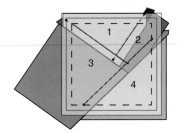

Foundation Piecing

String or chain piecing is sewing pieces together in a continuous string without clipping threads between sections.

String or Chain Piecing

Precuts: Cuts of fabric sold in packages by fabric manufacturers. Manufacturers have their own names for the different cuts but here are a few common sizes and terms.

- *Charms:* 5" squares (sometimes Nickels)
- *Layer Cakes:* 10" squares (sometimes Dimes)
- *Fat Eighth:* 9" x 22"
- *Fat Quarter:* 18" x 22"
- *Jelly Roll:* 2½" by width of fabric strips

Pressing: Pressing is the process of placing the iron on the fabric, lifting it off the fabric and placing it down in another location to flatten seams or crease fabric without sliding the iron across the fabric. Quilters do not usually use steam when pressing, since it can easily distort fabric shapes.

QST: Common abbreviation for quarter-square triangle.

Quilt (noun): A sandwich of two layers of fabric with a third insulating material between them that is then stitched together with the edges covered or bound.

Quilt (verb): Stitching several layers of fabric materials together with a decorative design. Stippling, crosshatch, channel, in-the-ditch, free-motion, allover and meandering are all terms for quilting designs.

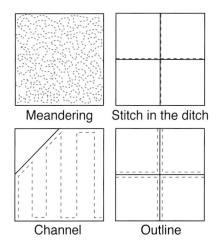

Quilt Sandwich: A layer of insulating material between a quilt's top and back fabric.

Quilting Skill Levels: Most quilting patterns will list a skill level that will help quilters decide if they have the skills to finish the quilt. Here are the most common:

- *Beginner:* A quilter who has been introduced to the basics of cutting, piecing and assembling a quilt top and is working to master these skills. Someone who has the knowledge of how to sandwich, quilt and bind a quilt, but may not have necessarily accomplished the task yet.
- *Confident Beginner:* A quilter who has pieced and assembled several quilt tops and is comfortable with the process, and is now ready to move on to more challenging techniques and projects using at least two different techniques.
- *Intermediate:* A quilter who is comfortable with most quilting techniques and has a good understanding of design, color and the quilting process. A quilter who is experienced in paper piecing, bias piecing and projects involving multiple techniques. Someone who is confident in making fabric selections other than those listed in the pattern.
- *Advanced:* A quilter who knows she or he can make any type of quilt and is looking for a challenging design. Someone who has the skills to read, comprehend and complete a pattern, and is willing to take on any technique. A quilter who is comfortable in her or his skills and has the ability to select fabric suited to the project.

Rotary Cutting: Using a rotary cutting blade and straightedge to cut fabric.

RS: Common abbreviation for right side of fabric.

Sashing: Strips of fabric sewn between blocks to separate or set off the designs.

Subcut: A second cutting of rotary-cut strips that makes the basic shapes used in block and quilt construction.

Template: A pattern made from a sturdy material which is then used to cut shapes for patchwork and appliqué quilting.

UFO: UnFinished Object

WOF: Common abbreviation for width of fabric.

WS: Common abbreviation for wrong side of fabric.

Annie's® *Learn to Make a Quilt From Start to Finish* is published by Annie's, 306 East Parr Road, Berne, IN 46711. Printed in USA. Copyright © 2014 Annie's. All rights reserved. This publication may not be reproduced in part or in whole without written permission from the publisher.

RETAIL STORES: If you would like to carry this pattern book or any other Annie's publication, visit AnniesWSL.com.

Every effort has been made to ensure that the instructions in this pattern book are complete and accurate. We cannot, however, take responsibility for human error, typographical mistakes or variations in individual work. Please visit AnniesCustomerCare.com to check for pattern updates.

ISBN: 978-1-57367-490-4
1 2 3 4 5 6 7 8 9